The Jacobson Joy Inventory

A New Look at Measuring Depression

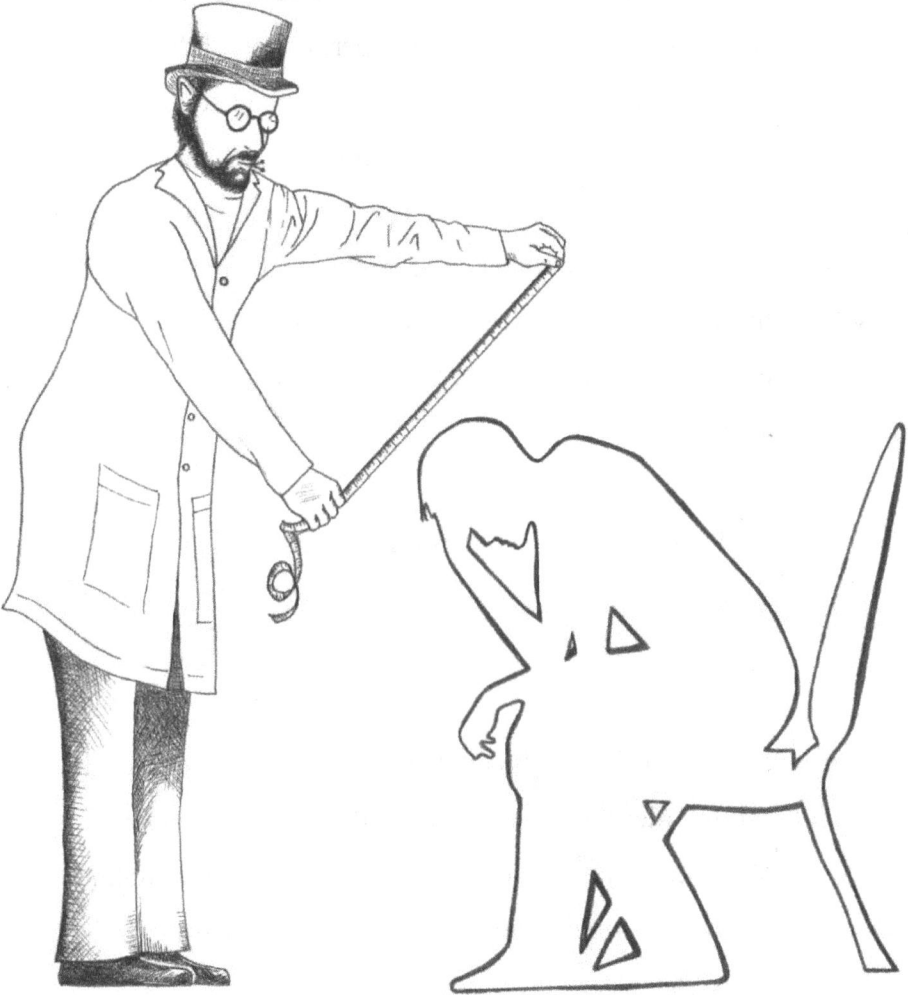

David M. Jacobson, LCSW, CHP

Cover: Shira S. Jacobson

ISBN-13:   978-0692839539 (Humor Horizons Publishing)
ISBN-10:   0692839534

This is a work of non-fiction all people places and events are for the most part real. In order for the measures in this book to be reliable they will need research testing so we'll have to wait for the weight of the measure to be measured. I am hopeful that these measures will be tested and that the tests will be measured.

CHAIR OF CONTENTS

I told my psychiatrist that everyone hates me.

He said I was being ridiculous - everyone hasn't met me yet.

Rodney Dangerfield

Sometimes the appropriate response to reality is to go insane.

Philip K. Dick

Dedication

This book is dedicated to those who assist those who live with depression and those with depression themselves.

PRE-FACE

For those who do not have a face yet, here is your pre-face.

If you're purchasing this guide in the hopes of cracking up while reading it, then you shouldn't get it. However, if you look forward to the possibility of this book putting a smile on your face, and even a chuckle at times, then I don't think you'll be disappointed. The purpose of this small guide is to offer clinicians (and any reader) another tool that may be helpful in measuring depression and dissipating its hold.

Give a man a fish and if he likes fish, he'll eat it; give a man a gourmet chef to cook the fish and he'll enjoy it much more. I hope this guide gives you a new recipe to consider using for your fish your treatment of depression. Though not intended for those seeking treatment, if that is you I hope you are encouraged to find a master chef of therapies to help you fry your own fish. Or something like that. All I'm trying to say is this is one more tool for your toolbox whether you are patient or practitioner. I hope you enjoy and find something that is helpful for you.

RECOGNITIONS

This part is typically called Acknowledgments, with the purpose to acknowledge and recognize others so I'm calling it Recognitions. I'd like to first recognize my editor. I've never had a real editor before; I've always just asked my brother Alan to look things over. Well, now I have an official editor, Kelly Epperson, so I am doing an official acknowledgement to thank her for her work in editing this guide.

I'd also like to thank the Association for Applied and Therapeutic Humor (AATH) for all that it/they and the board of directors have done for me in improving my knowledge base in therapeutic humor. I'm grateful for the many supportive colleagues and friendships I have made over the years as a result of belonging to this wonderful and humorous organization. There are too many to mention so I'll only name a few: Dr. Lee Berk, who has encouraged me to pursue the line of thinking presented in this guide; Mary Kay Morrison, President of the Association for Applied and Therapeutic Humor, who has always been supportive and has never lost touch in all the years we have known each other; Karyn Buxman, Ed Dunkelblau, Sporty King, Lenny Dave, Steve Sultanoff, Katherine Puckett, Chip Lutz and Nila Nielsen who along with Mary Kay, have taken AATH to a higher level of professionalism and without whom the organization may have withered away.

THE FAKE FOREWORD

This is a fake foreword for two reasons. One: Most forewords give you an introduction to the guide and tell you a lot about how great the book is and how great you are for wanting to read it. Two: A foreword is typically written by a person who is not the author. I'm writing my own foreword. But the book still is great and you are great for wanting to read it.

This fake foreword focuses on "four words" which I believe should have been the origin for the word foreword. Those four words are: Imagine if this were so.

Okay so I can't count that well. I probably should have said "Imagine this were so." It can be. Depression does not have to remain a way of life.

The point of this fake foreword is to respond to the critics that will flock to refute what this guide is about. They'll say "Where's the evidence? This is not an evidenced based practice!" Others may say "Why didn't I think of this?" or "What a great approach to use for measuring depression!" My approach here has not been used or researched by anyone but me. Because it has helped me, I believe it can help others.

Much of my struggle with depression was related to my self-doubts. Negative thinkers are stuck in an unhealthy balance of thoughts that are self-restrictive. Generating positive humorous thoughts is a continuous and ongoing process, and is actually hard work that pays off when you are determined to do it on a regular basis. Infusing positivity and humor into my life and work has made all the difference.

How willing are you or your clients to engage in self-management of thoughts? Ready to change? See the need to change? Have you weighed the pros and cons? Is there intention to change? I am optimistic because you are still reading. Read on, it won't hurt.

For those with depression: Now it's time for actions. These actions can become habits if repeated enough and maintained. Even if you relapse into negative thinking, you've already overcome your first hurdle because a relapse means you have made progress. You know what it's like to have positive thoughts and feelings, and you will have them again.

Reward yourself for positive actions and if you slip back into negative, say to yourself, "That's just great!" Let it go. (You can sing it if you want to, but if that song drives you nuts, then no singing.) Try to switch on the positive again. If relapsing, ask yourself: What do you think the problem is and why? What are you willing to try at this point? We are ALL always talking to ourselves so make your self-talk positive and productive. Use it to work for you, not against you.

They say the neon lights are bright on Broadway, but what if they run out of batteries? Humor is my battery, my energy charger that ensures that the lights stay on. If I had lost my sense of humor, I may have not still been here, either intentionally or by destructive behaviors. I can't speak for you, but I know humor pulled me out of a pit of darkness and rose me to the brightest of lights. The most important points I want to get across in this guide are that improvement is absolutely possible and that the two measurement tools I include here are not clinically validated at this time, but they work. They are measures I use for my personal self to gain a perspective of how well I am doing.

A score I'm unhappy with indicates that it's time to go into therapy or at the very least acknowledge that I am at a point where unhealthy thinking and behaviors are occurring and it's time to make a change. That in itself is incredibly helpful. I changed jobs as a result of taking these measures and I can tell you I am so much healthier and happier for doing it. This is my personal guide, not an evidence-based measure.

If you are a clinician that is interested in using it as an enhancement to your current tools, I encourage you to pursue research to test its validity and reliability. I will consider granting permission for any research proposals with this goal in mind.

My advice for clinician and client alike: Focus your time and energy on humor. Spending time on humor is utilizing time in a healthy way. Using your energy to bring humor to others strengthens your humor spirit. Having a strong humor spirit puts you in a strong position to increase rapport with others. If you work with clients, you'll be better able to help them cope with depressive thoughts and other nasty thoughts which lead to nasty feelings. If you're the guy with the nasty thoughts and feelings, humor will help you have less of that yuck and help you better able deal with everyone and everything around. Humor can help you return a healthier perspective. And give you hope. Hope keeps us hanging on.

If you think this fake foreword was a little different, wait until you read the Prologue.

PROLOGUE

I have never been against trees. However, I have at times been against logs. That is because a log is a symbol of a tree that was murdered. For you lumberjacks reading this, which I'm sure is my main audience, no I'm not a tree hugger. I'm too short and my arms aren't that long. And I know logs have nothing to do with prologues. This is opposed to pro-logs, people who are in favor of logs such as lumberjacks and others who work at saw mills and do a lot of "bucking." If you don't believe me, google the term. I'll wait.

Okay, I'll tell you. Bucking is the process for cutting felled trees into logs. The process for cutting a book into logs, er, chapters, is shown in the Table of Contents. You will not find a table of contents here. I thought a table was too big to put in this small guide so I used a Chair of Contents instead. This way, you can at least sit down while you're reading it. Instead of chapters, there are legs. They are there to keep the chair of contents up. Instead of chapter sections, there are floor protectors for each leg which act as the second part of the chapter or "leg."

Dr. Seuss has said, "I like nonsense, it wakes up the brain cells. Fantasy is a necessary ingredient in living. It's a way of looking at life through the wrong end of a telescope. Which is what I do, and that enables you to laugh at life's realities." Dr. Seuss was a wise man.

Back to the prologue. It is hoped that this guide will challenge you.

If you are a therapist, it will challenge you to stretch your therapeutic skill set to add therapeutic humor as an enhancement tool to your mental bag of interventions, theoretical frameworks and methods. If you are a therapist working with depressed clients, it will ask you to think about other ways to approach the issue of their depression. If you are a depressed person (that is, a therapist who became a therapist to deal with their own depression or a non-therapist who has a therapist who is dealing with their own depression or a person who just deals with depression), this guide will challenge you to look at your depression from another angle as well as encourage you to seek help. Seeking help takes courage and it's better to be a brave depressive who will seek help than a cowardly one who gives up because "so far" nothing has worked.

Disclaimer: This guide is not intended to treat depression. The author is not responsible for you being even more depressed after reading it, though the hope is that you could possibly be a little less depressed, a little more optimistic, and more open to seeking help and improving the quality of your life; and if you're a clinician, that you'll be open to new tools all the time.

Datclaimer: Datclaimer is like a dis claimer, but it's different because it's the second claimer which makes it a dat claimer. Enough of dis and dat, this guide doesn't claim anything. It does hopes that it can be a help-you guide. I say help you because it is not a self-help guide; as the author I am the self and you are not myself so it cannot be a self-help guide to anyone but me. To you, it could be a help-you guide if in fact it actually helps you go in the right direction.

As Buddha said, always take the Middle Road. When he was on the Middle Road, he stopped at a hot dog stand and said, "Make me one with everything." The vendor made him one with everything and said, "That'll be $2.00." Buddha gave him a $5.00 bill. The vendor smiled and sat back down. Buddha asked, "Where's my change?" The hot dog vendor replied, "Change must come from within."

And so it is for you or those you wish to help. There must be at least an inkling of desire to improve the situation or there is not much hope for change. Your reading further is an indication that there is hope for change whether for your clients or for yourself.

Enough of this banter; let's get into the guide.

WELCOME

I would venture to guess that if you are reading this, you either have experienced depression yourself or have known others that have, or are a clinician or other health care professional that treats and assists others with depression; (and then there will be the occasional hospital clown or pet food tester that just felt like reading something different for a change). The vast majority of humans fall into one of these categories (except clowns and pet food testers) and if you're reading this there is a very high probability that you are a human.

I'm a fellow human. A little about me: My father died when I was eight years old, I was physically abused after his death, all my grandparents had died by the time I was eighteen, I was diagnosed with severe arthritis at age twenty-two and have lived with chronic sometimes debilitating pain ever since. I also became addicted to drugs to deal with the pain, (but have long since overcame the addiction.) And did I mention I was depressed?

Celebrities often get tagged as the face of whatever cause they are involved with; think of:

Jerry Lewis, the face of Muscular Dystrophy

Liz Taylor, the face of AIDS

Michael J Fox, the face of Parkinson's disease

Christopher Reeves, the face of spinal cord injury.

I'm not famous enough to be the face of depression, but perhaps I may someday be the ass of arthritis....

Did I have reasons to be depressed? I think so, but is my normal state depressive? No, not at all. Perhaps that is a gift at least partially due to my genetics, but there is another reason. My sense of humor. My normal state is not depressed; my normal state of being is contentment and happiness. That I attribute to my sense of humor. Not only has it kept me alive, but it has helped me enormously to thrive.

There are those with depression that may need medication to help balance their brain chemistry in addition to one of the evidenced based treatments that have been found to helpful. For the rest of us though, if that is not the case, then I think this guide can help you. My daily silly thoughts energize me and help me enjoy my day. My use of humor has helped me through depression, chronic pain, and everyday life, personally and professionally.

A good sense of humor can't cure all ailments, but data is mounting about the positive things that humor and laughter can do.

There are long-tail benefits and short-term effects. We all know a good laugh has great immediate results. When you start to laugh, it doesn't just lighten your load mentally, it actually induces physical changes in your body.

Laughter can stimulate organs. If you own a piano or an organ and it doesn't sound right, laughter may help tune it. Okay, that's not true, but laughter enhances your intake of oxygen-rich air, stimulates your heart, lungs and muscles. A good laugh eases tension in the room and in your body. Laughter can also stimulate circulation and aid muscle relaxation, both of which can help reduce some of the physical symptoms of stress. Everybody can use a dose of that.

Laughing together, or "suffering" together, is better than doing it alone. One of my closest friends, Kevin, has the more "glamorous" arthritis, rheumatoid, as opposed to my inferior type as he calls it, psoriatic arthritis. The funny thing is we commiserate about our suffering together and do it all with no pity or begging for sympathy; we just treat these pains as fact and move on. Just knowing we share some challenges together is helpful.

Knowing you're not alone makes everything easier, and that is the bridge that humor provides. Every day occurrences can turn humorous if you're wearing your humor hat. For example, my wife took our 16-year-old son to urgent care. She texted me that they think it might be mono. Then she texted that they "were doing the blood prick now." I responded that I hate when they take blood from your …. well, you know. It made them both laugh and the urgent care visit a little more tolerable.

Depending on how severe one's depression is, humor can make depression a little more tolerable too.

What we get out of life is not determined by the good feelings we desire, but by the bad feelings we're willing and able to sustain until you get to the good feelings.

When your friends find out you are depressed they may offer you some advice like: Lighten Up! Don't worry, be happy! (Because maybe that never occurred to you?) They mean well, but such advice usually does not help.

When any other organ in your body gets sick, you get sympathy, but if the organ happens to be your brain, people don't know how to handle it. The brain is a pretty complex organism. In fact, it ultimately decides whether you are going to end up harming yourself or holding out for a better solution. My hope is that you hold out for a better solution. I mean who knows what you may do with your life. What if you turn out to be the next George Bailey? For you youngsters that may not have seen it You don't really know do you? I know the change that has happened with me, so I have hope for you.

POSTLOGUE

This is the part in the guide that should follow the pre-logue. I guess we didn't have that; we had the pro-logue and the pre-face and the welcome…. No matter….

One of the goals of this guide is to shift to a more positive way of thinking. What do positive humor spirit thoughts say to you? "Don't pass gas loud enough to be heard." "If you sneeze, make sure no boogers are stuck on you." "Don't walk around with poo on your pants. Don't fall off the stage while speaking. Don't jump up and down screaming while holding your groin. Don't talk to a large audience with your fly opened." (I have done all these things.) And are any of those statements positive? Or are they more laced with worry? Have you ever thought about your thoughts?

What prompts your negative thoughts? When you watch too much negative news or read the paper and focus on the negative stories, do you start to worry and become afraid? Does an election result worry you? It doesn't have to be all gloom and doom. With a little effort, you can shift from negative to positive. Have you ever looked at newspaper headlines and tried to see how funny they can be by reframing the meaning?
Here are some examples:

- Police Begin Campaign To Run Down Jaywalkers
- Farmer Bill Dies In House

- Is There A Ring Of Debris Around Uranus?

- Prostitutes Appeal to Pope

- Panda Mating Fails: Veterinarian Takes Over

- Enraged Cow Injures Farmer with Ax

- War Dims Hope For Peace

- If Strike Isn't Settled Quickly, It May Last a While

- Red Tape Holds Up New Bridge

- Man Struck By Lightning Faces Battery Charge

- New Study Of Obesity Looks For Larger Test Group

- Local High School Dropouts Cut In Half

- Steals Clock, Faces Time

- Sex Education Delayed, Teachers Request Training

- Queen Mary Having Bottom Scraped

-Tiger Woods Plays with Own Balls, Nike says

-Alton attorney accidently sues himself

-County to pay $250,000 to advertise lack of funds

Certainly at least one of these headlines made you smile. If you look for these types of slips of the tongue, you're bound to find some positive humor spirit. Positive humor is everywhere; we just have to look for it.

It begins with paying attention to what you pay attention to - negative or positive. What would happen if you skipped your negative thought-provoking habits for a few days a week? How many more positive thoughts would you have because of this minor change? Do you experience any repetitive thoughts that occur over and over? Do you experience any repetitive thoughts that occur over and over? Do you experience any repetitive thoughts that occur over and over? (Sorry, couldn't resist.) Do you get caught in a negative loop? "What's my financial situation today? I better worry about money again, because I haven't worried about my financial situation since yesterday!"

Seriously, how important is attitude?

A young couple, just married, were in their honeymoon suite on their wedding night. As they were undressing for bed, the husband -- who was a big burly man -- tossed his trousers to his bride and said, "Here, put these on." She put them on and the waist was twice the size of her body.

"I can't wear your trousers," she said.

"That's right," said the husband, "and don't you ever forget it. I'm the man who wears the pants in this family."

With that, she flipped him her panties and said, "Try these on."

He tried and found he could only get them on as far as his kneecaps.

"Hell," he said. "I can't get into your panties!"

She replied, "That's right, and that's the way it's going to stay until your attitude changes."

INTRODUCTION

I offer a challenge to my mental health colleagues, fellow psychotherapists, and social workers; those with an interest in mental health; and those who experience problems with living. In other words, all of us. If you have been diagnosed with a mental illness, you, like all human beings, fall into the third category - problems with living. There are none on this planet that I know of that do not fall into this category. Even Mother Theresa admitted that she had problems with living. No one is perfect. Not saints, not sinners and certainly not mental health professionals. With that in mind, I challenge all who read this guide to look at depression and other "problems with living" from a different angle – the angle of a therapeutic humorist perspective.

As a Certified Humor Professional, (yes, that actually is a designation; go to AATH.org to learn more), I am as proud of my CHP designation as I am of my Licensed Clinical Social Worker (LCSW) designation. There are many other designations and names I've been called, but I won't share them here as they do not do much to help my self-esteem.

Why is my CHP and use of therapeutic humor important? As a psycho-therapist and former supervisor of 18 mental health programs and 200 psycho-therapists and social workers, I've found that the key to helping others lies in the ability to build rapport. Nothing builds rapport like having the ability to sit with another human being and have a chuckle together. That is the basis of spiritual connections that are revealed to those who reach a mastery of the humor spirit.

In the movie "Rain Man," the two most important moments to me were when "Rain Man" said "Charlie Babbitt made a joke" and Rain Man got the joke. It is the only time in the whole movie when Rain Man chuckled and in that moment showed he had insight into humor. It was a connection on a spiritual level that led them to the second moment when Rain Man and his brother Charlie Babbitt touched heads together. That connection is a divine gift and if you are able to connect with another soul in such a way, you are on par with the great Yogi Masters of the world. Humor is just one spiritual element to use to obtain such a connection. There are many others such as love, but I have difficulty distinguishing between love and humor as to me they are two sides of the same coin.

I have lived with chronic pain for nearly four decades now and the reason I have thrived in all this time is due to my sense of humor and the power of humor to overcome adversity. This is the school of learning from which I speak. My real education was not from my college years, and not from a piece of paper that says I am a LCSW, although I respect that designation. For all of us, the real school is life. To have the ability to overcome adversity may come from many places. For me it comes from the spirit of humor. My wish is that you too can develop your sense of humor to a point where it can help you and also allow you to help others cope with problems of living.

I know if I lost my sense of humor I would lose my reason for being here. For that reason, I am vigilant and unbending in my need to use humor every day of my life. My best friend, David Lempert, is the same way. We made a vow to each other many years ago to make others laugh every day of our lives, and so far neither one of us has failed in our mission.

Leg One: Depression

There are many books about depression. That in itself is depressing. The words used to describe depression are very depressing:

"How are you feeling?"

"Oh, I'm just feeling a little sad, tired, troubled, angry, irritable, and frustrated and have no interest in anything and just want to isolate myself from the world."

"Gee, you sound like you may be depressed?"

"No, I feel fine."

Let's tell the truth. There are many people who are depressed and know they are depressed. They just don't know what to do about it. There are many effective treatments for depression. Treatment can be accomplished by someone (a therapist for example) that you have a good relationship with or can build a good relationship with. The best addition to any treatment is your connection to another human being. For me, that connection is based on the use of therapeutic humor.

A person with a great sense of humor can reach out and connect with others. What most people need when they are depressed is to re-connect with those they care about or can learn to care about. Everyone needs to have someone or something as reasons for getting out of their funk. There may be bio-chemical reasons for depression, life experiences that can cause depression, and a combination of both and other issues that can make depression worse. What improves someone's outlook? Hope. Hope brought on by healthy satisfying relationships. Hope by discovering you can enjoy doing things either alone or with others. An example of doing something alone may be reading this guide. There are other creative uses you can do with this guide. For example, you can read this guide out loud to a three-year-old child that you want to put to sleep.

Since Leg One is titled Depression, let's go on to figuring out how depressed we really are.

Floor Protector for Leg One: Thinking about depression.

Giving credit where credit is due, I would like to acknowledge the role that cognitive therapy plays in this guide. In my book, *The 7 ½ Habits of Highly Humorous People*, I wrote about the half habit of changing your thought processes and re-framing how you see the world. I'm not going to go in depth with cognitive restructuring, but one of the first things to be done is identifying automatic thoughts. Automatic thoughts are thoughts you have that you do not need to engage a clutch to have. Ha ha. No one these days seems to know how to drive a car with a clutch. Anyway…

Automatic thoughts are thoughts you may not be conscious of, but they're running inside you all the time. Automatic thoughts are not necessarily the truth. For example: You walk by someone and say hello; they do not respond. Your inner automatic thought says, "How rude, they must not like me." The reality could be that they didn't hear you or they have a bad stomach ache or they were preoccupied worrying about their bank account balance or they think you work for the CIA or a dozen other possibilities. We just typically go to the automatic – "they don't like me," even though that could be the farthest thing from the truth.

This therapy tool of becoming aware of your automatic thoughts can be used to decrease depressive thoughts. How quickly and effectively you open up to this can be contingent on the rapport and relationship between client and therapist. If you don't have a therapist, then it is contingent on how well you can catch yourself while thinking automatic thoughts. Cognitive therapies like noticing and changing your automatic thoughts can be used to decrease your depression and increase your quality of life.

Therapeutic humor can enhance this therapy by twisting the thoughts in a humorous direction and making them fun so you can more easily see how silly some thoughts can be. To illustrate the point, after the Tucson Shooting Tragedy, there were some people that were so traumatized by the event that they couldn't enter a grocery store anymore because the shooting occurred outside of a store. The automatic thought became "If I go to the grocery store, someone might shoot me."

I had one client who we will call Fannie who had such automatic thoughts that led to a new belief that grocery stores are not safe. I asked "Fannie" if grocery stores were safer than fighting in Iraq or Afghanistan. She looked at me puzzled. I explained that you don't have to go grocery shopping when you're in the army, so being in the army must be safer. This made her chuckle a little and she said, "I guess our grocery stores are safer than being in Iraq or Afghanistan." Therapeutic humor is a powerful tool that can be used to put things in perspective. Countless examples can be used to help someone reframe their thoughts.

A veteran, "Dan," I was working with on dealing with his PTSD had a traumatic brain injury as a result of a trauma from being snuck up on and struck in the head from behind and knocked out. He also had a thing about stores saying he couldn't wait in any line because someone behind him could strike him in the head. You may think this sounds silly, but we all have thoughts that when brought to the light of day seem a little off. But to the person, they are very real and keep them from fully living life. I suggested Dan just try shopping once and when in line, turn to the person behind him and ask them if they were going to hit him in the head. Dan took a chance and went into the store. He selected an item and got in the check-out line. When Dan was in line, he turned toward the person behind him smiling at the thought of asking her that question. The woman smiled back and started a conversation with him. Through Dan's humorous imagination of asking the fellow shopper if she was going to hit him on the head, he was able to begin shopping again. I'm not saying it's always that simple, but it does show the power of therapeutic humor in relation to cognitive therapies.

Think of depression like water and all the particles it contains. Think of your thoughts as some of the particles that are in the water. If you want cleaner water or cleaner thoughts, then the thoughts must go through a filtration purification process just as a water filter removes the debris from water. In order to cleanse your thoughts, you must be aware of what they contain. If they have arsenic and old lace in them, you must have a way to remove the arsenic and use the old lace to make yourself gloves to warm some of your thoughts.

CPT (Cognitive Processing Therapy) is an effective evidence based treatment used by therapists in the VA to treat PTSD. The first step is to identify your thoughts and feelings, then to challenge those thoughts that are distorted and not reflective of reality. For example: "The world is a dangerous and terrifying place. Everything in the world is dangerous." This is a global statement rather than the reality that at times the world is dangerous, but at other times there can be joyful moments and safe and comfortable times as well. You may then instead think the world is sometimes a dangerous place but my life is not threatened 24 hours a day 7 days a week. With therapeutic humor, you could tell yourself: There are things in the world that are not necessarily dangerous. Toilet paper, for example. "I do not think of toilet paper as dangerous, therefore "Everything" is not dangerous."

"Hi, Hank, how was your day?"

"Well, it was pretty good, except when I was in the bathroom I saw a roll of toilet paper and it scared me."

If you think that is just silly, then think about the statement that the world is a dangerous place and everything in the world is dangerous. Now could that statement be silly?

"Stuck points" are points where we often seem to get stuck, a tool used in Cognitive Processing Therapy. For example: I used to hate pens and could never use them, but then I realized they have a point! Hmm. Not a great example, let's try another: The reason I'm depressed is because of Jed I. Knight. So it's Jed I. Knight's fault that I am depressed. That blame you put on Jed I. could be keeping you stuck from going on with your life. At this point you could ask yourself some challenging questions. If you say to yourself "I should have known better than to let Jed I. talk me into going to Tatooine." Ask yourself, why should I have known? Am I psychic? Can I predict everything that is going to happen? If this method of challenging yourself interests you, consider seeing a therapist who uses cognitive processing therapy if you have experienced severe traumas in your life.

I have used these challenging questions myself to get passed my stuck points. For example. *Distorted thought: If I never got arthritis, I would have been an Olympian athlete. Challenging question: What if I was an Olympian athlete? Then I would have never gone to graduate school for social work and become a Chief or Director responsible for improving the lives of countless others who have struggled with their problems with living. Also as a famous Olympian I would have attracted a stalker who could have killed me.*

In that case the only reason I am still alive is because I got arthritis. Maybe a silly way of looking at it, but it's much better than living my life feeling I lost out on some other destiny and focusing my whole life on what could have been versus celebrating all the things in my life that I am grateful for.

What are you telling yourself that reinforces your depression? I guessing it's not "I am great and so proud of all of my accomplishments." It's probably more focusing on every failure that you have experienced. It's kind of like when you get a car and all of a sudden you see the same make and model everywhere. They were always there, you just didn't focus on noticing them before. So it is with your accomplishments and your sense of humor. Both have always been there, you just never focused on them before.

Here's a little story: Once there was a King and Queen who live in a Queendom (that's for you feminists out there) where all the people were depressed. The King was depressed, the queen was depressed. Even the court jester was depressed. Then one day a social worker came to the Queendom. The social worker asked for an audience with the King and Queen and when meeting them asked, "Why is everyone depressed here?"

The queen answered, "There are many reasons. For some of us, it's our genetics, others have had many losses, and then there are others that were abused by myself and the King. The rest, I guess, just wanted to fit in so they too became depressed."

27

The social worker said, "I'm a cognitive behavioral therapist and I think I can change this whole Queendom if you are willing to change."

The King and Queen thought about this offer and then decided to behead the social worker and continue as they were. The moral of the story if you're a clinician is don't ever visit that Queendom. Seriously, many just can't see any way out of their depression.

No one can or should be expected to just "snap out of it." That's a very frustrating thing to say to someone with depression. With major depressions, even brief moments of joy may not be possible. I'm talking about my personal experience and even when I was depressed, there were some advantages to it. We think our depression is somehow keeping us safe. It came to a point where the disadvantages outweighed any advantages and I realized I had a choice on how to view my situation from another angle. It was my sense of humor that helped me come to this conclusion. For example, before the arthritis I used to walk with a bounce in my stride like Tigger. That's T-I-double "guh"-errrrr, that spells Tigger! With the arthritis, when I finally could get up and walk again, I initially was hunched over and could only take tiny steps with the feel of walking bare foot over glass. This was very depressing so I thought "If I have to walk like this I should at least have a little fun with it and began walking like Igor, the hunchback. I still had to walk funny, but at least now it was funny to me and others as well.

In the next Leg, I'm going to propose that we measure depression from a different angle.

Leg Two: The Jacobson Joy Inventory©

The best answer to the question "How sad are you?" is "I'm not sad."

The best answer to the question "How happy are you?" is "I'm very happy."

To the first question, the worst answer would be "I'm extremely sad;" as opposed to the worst answer to the second question being "I'm not happy at all."

So, would you rather say "I'm not happy at all" or would you rather say "I'm extremely sad"?

How do you feel saying *I'm not happy at all* versus saying *I'm extremely sad*? My guess is you would not feel as bad saying the first reply. At least we are still talking about being happy. When we take depression tests, we can feel even more depressed after taking it. If the questions were worded differently maybe you wouldn't feel as bad, but you would still know you have a problem to address. That is the whole point of this guide and my measurement tool. Some may say it's just semantics, but words play a powerful role in shaping how we feel about ourselves. For example, unlawful shopping doesn't sound so bad, but it's still stealing.

Many clients understand the concept: "If I want to change the way I feel, I have to change the way I think". The same holds true for clinicians. If I expect my clients to change the way they think, it is better for me to present them with measures that encourage the change in their thought processes to a more positive perspective. That means using more positive words.

We have to ask: What emotions are clients feeling after completing a depression measure? Do the questions in the measure move them towards healing or reinforcing how depressed they may be?

What follows are two ways to try to ascertain the level of depression one experiences but in a way that perhaps the person will not feel as depressed after obtaining the results.

The Jacobson Joy Inventory© is a measure of depression based on how much or how little joy one is experiencing at the present moment. Our thoughts and feelings are constantly changing, therefore you can expect the results of this measure to also vary depending on present mood.

Jacobson's Joy Inventory is a 21-Question Inventory to assess happiness and depression created with positive verbiage from a Therapeutic Humor perspective. I remind you that this is NOT an Evidenced Based Measure and has not been researched by others to verify its validity or reliability. Those interested in using it for research purposes are encouraged to do so by requesting the author's permission.

The theory and hope is that after taking this assessment a person or practitioner may be able to generally gauge the level of depression or happiness and the person will not feel as bad as they would if taking a different type of depression measure.

Jacobson's Joy Inventory Mood Assessment:

Since your last visit, have you felt happy most of the time or even some of the time?

1. Happiness

3) I never feel happy

2) I am rarely happy

1) I am happy sometimes

0) I feel happy much of the time

2. Optimism

3) I am never optimistic about the future

2) Though I can experience optimism, it is rare for me

1) I feel more encouraged about my future than I used to

0) I expect things to work out for me

3. Past Success

3) I never feel successful

2) I have experienced success in the past, but have had more failures

1) As I look back, I see a lot of successes, but not as much as I'd like

0) I feel I am a success as a person

4. Increase in Joy

3) I do not experience joy

2) I enjoy things, but not very often

1) I experience joy, but would like to have more joy in my life

0) There is plenty of joy in my life

5. Mistakes

3) I have made too many mistakes in my life and dwell on them

2) I have made mistakes and things remind me of them

1) I have made some mistakes, but I can live with them.

0) My mistakes don't stop me from moving forward

6. Reward feelings

3) I don't feel deserving of any rewards

2) I haven't done anything yet to be rewarded for

1) I sometimes feel I deserve recognition

0) I look forward to many rewards in the future

7. Self-liking

3) I wish I was somebody else, but I don't know who?

2) Sometimes I'm ok being me

1) I am sometimes confident in myself, but not as confident as I'd like to be

0) I like being me

8. Praise

3) I don't deserve praise

2) I rarely deserve praise

1) I would like to feel deserving of praise more often

0) I am often praised or feel praised

9. Purpose

3) I have no life purpose, no reason to live

2) I rarely feel a reason to live

1) I feel I have reasons enough to live to keep me going

0) I have a purposeful life

10. Laughter and tears

3) I cry lot and never laugh

2) I cry more than I laugh

1) I sometimes cry and sometimes laugh, but wish I would laugh more

0) I laugh more than I cry

11. Tranquility

3) I never feel peaceful

2) I have felt peaceful, but it's rare

1) I sometimes feel peaceful

0) I feel peaceful more than not

12. Interest

3) I don't have interests

2) I rarely have interests

1) I am sometimes interested in things

0) Life is for the most part interesting

13. Decision making

3) It's very hard to make any decisions

2) I can make decisions, but it's not easy

1) I usually need some help making decisions

0) Decisions can be an exciting challenge for me

14. Worthiness

3) I am never worthy

2) I rarely feel worthy as a person

1) I sometimes feel worthy as a person, but more often not

0) I live a worthwhile life

15. Energy

3) I don't have any energy

2) I rarely have enough energy to do things

1) I sometimes have energy to do things

0) I am happy with my energy level

16. Sleep

3) I can rarely sleep or I always seem to be sleeping

2) I sleep, but either not enough or too much

1) I sleep pretty well but still a little too much/ not quite enough

0) I'm happy with the amount of sleep I get

17 Cheerfulness

3) I am never cheerful

2) I am rarely cheerful

1) I am cheerful sometimes

0) I'm cheerful more than I am not

18. Appetite

3) I always /or never want to eat

2) I eat too much/ or rarely feel like eating

1) I sometimes eat too much/ sometimes lose my appetite

0) I usually enjoy my meals

19. Focus

3) I never can seem to focus

2) I can focus, but it's hard

1) I can focus but not as well as I'd like

3) I focus just fine, thank you

20. Alertness

3) I never feel wide awake/ or I am always on alert

2) I'm usually very tired or usually too alert

1) I'm not as alert as I'd like to be

0) I happy with my alertness level

21 Sex interest

3) I'm never interested in sex

2) I'm rarely interested in sex

1) I'm not as interested in sex as I'd like to be

0) I'm content with my level of interest in sex

Raw Scores

29-63 Indicates severe depression at this current time, but there are treatments to decrease depression

20-28 Indicates moderate depression but there is reason for optimism

14-19 Indicates mild depression, but some happiness as well

8-13 Healthy level of happiness and depression

0-7 Very content with life

Floor Protector for Leg Two: The PHQ or Positive Health Questionnaire©.

[Again, this is not an Evidenced Based Measure. Those interested in using it for research purposes are encouraged to do so with permission of course. I welcome your inquiries.]

Over the last 2 weeks, rate how you experience the following:

	Not at all	Several Days	More than half the days	Nearly every day
1. Pleasure in doing things	3	2	1	0
2. Feeling up, happy, or hopeful	3	2	1	0
3. Sleeping well	3	2	1	0
4. Feeling energetic	3	2	1	0
5. Normal appetite - not too much /not	3	2	1	0

too little				
6. Feeling good about yourself	3	2	1	0
7. Good concentration -watching television, reading, other things	3	2	1	0
8. Moving / speaking normal.	3	2	1	0
9. Neither restless or too sluggish	3	2	1	0
10. Thoughts that you have reasons to live, that you are safe	3	2	1	0
If you checked any	Not difficult at	Somewhat	Very	Extremely

3s, how difficult have these made it for you to do your work, take care of things at home or get along with other people?	all 0	difficult 1	difficult 2	difficult 3

Interpreting the results of the completed Positive Health Questionnaire©:

If there are at least 5 checks in the number 3 section or if the answer to questions one and two were both in the number 3 "Not at All" column, therapy is strongly recommended.

If there are at least 4 checks in the number 3 column, therapy is still recommended.

Since the questionnaire relies on the honesty of the person taking it to be truthful with their answers, all responses should be verified by an objective observer such as a clinician or those who know the person well for a definitive conclusion about the level of depression experienced. The questionnaire is dependent on how seriously the person taking the measure addressed it and how realistic their responses really are.

Another important note, if the answer to question #10 is zero, the person should seek help immediately and call 800-273-8233 and tell the person on the phone that when asked if they have any reason to live they could not come up with any.

There are exceptions to the rule of course: normal bereavement after a loved one passes away, a history of experiencing great excitement, hyperactivity or an actual physical disorder, medication, or other drugs as the biological cause of symptoms.

Any mental health diagnosis requires a clinical evaluation by a licensed behavioral health professional; this guide is not such a person. In fact, it is not even a person, it is a guide, a dead tree remnant as you may recall from the foreword. It may also be a digital version of a guide.

To monitor severity over time, complete the questionnaires at times when you/client are in a normal state and then repeat at regular intervals (e.g., every 2 weeks) to see if there are any changes. If in therapy, scores should improve over time.

Add up checks by column.

Add together column scores to get a TOTAL score.

Interpretation of Total Score:

Total Score   Depression / Happiness

0-1   Very Happy Person

2-4   Happy and content

5-9   Minimal/mild depression

10-14   Moderate depression seek help

15-19   Moderately to severe depression seek more help

20-30 Severe depression [Call 800-273-8233]

Leg Three: Summary

Okay, so it's a three-legged Chair of Contents.

Therapeutic Humor can be a powerful tool to assist a clinician in strengthening the therapeutic bond through improved building of rapport. Humor can enhance an individual's ability to improve their cognitions, feelings and physical wellness. Humor can revitalize one's sense of humor and sense of playfulness. Humor can create resiliency through the use of finding humorous insights ("Charlie Babbitt made a joke") and discovering things about the self in a non-defensive way through humor, amusement and play.

For an in-depth look at humor in clinical social work, read Stephanie Nathanson's DSW dissertation: *A Two-Paper Examination on The Integration Of Humor Into Clinical Social Work.* University of Pennsylvania.

Okay, I'm going to stop now because if I add much more, it's going to turn into a book instead of a guide and I don't have time to write a whole book at this time. Besides I wouldn't know what to title it, if it were a book instead of a guide. How about *A Book Without A Title*?

The Book Without A Title. Kind of like who's on first…

Have you read *The Book Without A Title*?

What book without a title?

You know, *The Book Without A Title*.

Does it have a title?

Yes.

What is it?

The Book Without A Title.

I know but does it have a title?

Yes!

Let me try again, what is the title of the book without a title?

The Book Without A Title.

That's the name of the book?

No. *That's The Name of The Book* is a different book.

If I picked up the book you are referring to and looked at the cover, what would I see?

The title of the book.

Ah hah! So what would it say?

The Book Without A Title.

Exactly what I thought!

Enough of that. I thank you for reading and I welcome your feedback. If you are in a helping profession, you may wish to consider joining the Association for Applied and Therapeutic

Humor. Also consider applying for the Humor Academy to become a Certified Humor Professional yourself. Visit AATH.org for more details.

Floor Protector for Leg Three: Other Random ADHD thoughts.

For clinicians only...

Ah screw it. If you're not a clinician, go ahead and read on too.

Psychoneuroimmunology and Humor: Evidence is growing year by year that your thoughts, moods, emotions, and belief system have a fundamental impact on the body's basic health and healing mechanisms and general state of wellness.

Questions to ask your clients:

What do I like about who I am?

What am I good at? What skills and talents do I have?

What positive characteristics do I have?

What have I achieved in my life; my accomplishments?

What are the successes in my life?

What are some challenges I have overcome?

What do others say they like about me?

What are some attributes I like in others that I also have in common?

How might someone who cared about me describe me?

What do I think my friends like best about me?

What we think is tremendously important. We have the power to reprogram our thoughts to be more positive and optimistic. Humor goes a long way in improving our thought patterns and our emotions. Follow the link below to see the chart "Potential ways in which humor can contribute to recovery" from Marc Gelkopf's article, The Use of Humor in Serious Mental Illness: A Review Evid Based Complement Alt Med. 2011: 342837.

https://www.hindawi.com/journals/ecam/2011/342837/

Having less negative and distorted thoughts can go a long way to treat depression. As will less anxiety, less shame, less stress and the instillment of hope. Reframing our words, our thoughts, our view of life is the key to keeping depression at bay. That starts now. That is my very objective here.

It is my goal that you will see the importance of humor in dealing with any situation, and especially depression. Implementing humor can become a natural part of your day and you will see that it improves rapport and morale. Any little bit of bright lining in a day can keep a person going. It is also my goal that you see I am serious about being silly and I am serious about keeping a positive attitude in all matters, including how we take measurements of depression. If a client can take a test and get results without feeling even worse, that has to be an improvement for all concerned.

My Jacobson's Joy Inventory is one tool. Humor is a tool. Be open to all the tools available to treat depression. This small guide is just the tip of the iceberg. There are so many ways to further your study of therapeutic humor. Just a few of which are mentioned in the

Resource section of this guide. I encourage you to join me in this quest.

I'll see you in the funny papers.

ABOUT THE AUTHOR

David Jacobson, MSW, LCSW, author, speaker, social worker, administrator, husband, father, friend, is the owner of Humor Horizons and is the Director of Behavioral Health Case Management at Banner University Medical Center South. David presents keynotes and workshops on humor and health, communication, leadership, team building and stress reduction all in a fun and entertaining way. He is the former manager of social work at University Medical Center and worked with patients and families of traumas including the tragic shooting event in Tucson that happened in January 8, 2011.

Jacobson's many honors include a "President's Award" from FlashNet Marketing, Inc., A "National Hero" award and a Lifetime Achievement award from the Arthritis Foundation National Office, and the 1997 Wayne Washburn Memorial Award which reads as follows "We all need someone or something to inspire us to bring out our best. You are that someone."

Connect with David at www.humorhorizons.org.

RESOURCES

In addition to the dissertation previously mentioned, here are some more references for further reading.

- Buxman, Karyn. *Amazed and Amused: How to Survive and Thrive as a Healthcare Professional;* series *What's So Funny About . . . (Diabetes, Heart Disease, Nursing . . .)*
- Cousins, Norman. *Anatomy of an Illness*
- Epperson, Kelly. *365 Days of Joy; When Life Stinks, It's Time to Wash the Gym Clothes*
- Glickman, David. *Punchline Your Bottom Line (76 Ways To Get Any Business Audience Laughing)*
- King, Sporty. *I Found Out I'm Dying: A Celebration of Life in Spoetry; S.T.U.F.F. Happens; Morning . . . Noon . . . & Night; Your Name Came to Mind*
- Klein, Allen. The Courage to Laugh: Humor, Hope, and Healing in the Face of Death and Dying; Healing Power of Humor; You Can't Ruin My Day, Always Look on the Bright Side; L.A.U.G.H.
- Kuhn M.D., Clifford It All Starts with a Smile: 7 Steps to Being Happier Right Now
- Kwan, Jacki. *Almost Home*
- Laurenhue, Kathy. *Getting to Know the Life Stories of Older Adults: Activities for Building Relationships; Alzheimer's Basic Caregiving – an ABC Guide*
- Lutz, Chip. *Leadership by the Numbers*

- Martin, Rod A. *The Psychology of Humor: An Integrative Approach*
- McGhee, Paul. *Health, Healing and the Amuse System*
- Morrison, Mary Kay. *Using Humor to Maximize Living; Using Humor to Maximize Learning*
- Moss, Bob Hubba Jubba. *The Enthusiasm–Laffter Connection: A Guide for Gaining Positive Life Skills*
- Passanisi, Kathleen. *It's Your Life; Choose Well*
- Ravich, Lenny. *A Funny Thing Happened on the Way to Enlightenment*
- Schwartz, Enid. *Humor in Healthcare: the Laughter Prescription*
- Schwartz, Joel L, MD. *Noses Are Red – How to Nurture Your Child's Sense of Humor; To Pee or Not to Pee . . .*
- Sparks, Susan, The Rev. *Laugh Your Way to Grace: Reclaiming the Spiritual Power of Humor*
- Trout, Shirley. *Light Dances: Illuminating Families with Laughter and Love*
- Wooten, Patty. *Compassionate Laughter: Jest for Your Health; Heart, Humor and Healing and Compassionate Laughter*
- Wilson, Steve. Eat Dessert First; Super Humor Power

There are several papers and articles as well:

- Berk, L.S., Tan, S.A., Fry, W.F., Napier, B.J., Lee, J.W.,

Hubbard, R.W., Lewis, J.E., and Eby, W.C. (1989) Neuroendrocrine and stress hormone changes during mirthful laughter. American Journal of the Medical Sciences, 298(6), 390-396.

- Bloch S, Browning S, McGrath G. Humour in group psychotherapy. *British Journal of Medical Psychology*. 1983;56(1):89–97

- Farrelly F, Lynch M. Humor in provocative therapy. In: Fry WF Jr, Salameh WA, editors. *Handbook of Humor and Psychotherapy: Advances in the Clinical Use of Humor*. Sarasota, Fla, USA: Professional Resource Exchange; 1987. pp. 81–106.

- Fry, W.F. (1992) The physiologic effects of humor, mirth, and laughter. *Journal of the American Medical Association*, 267(13), 1857-1858.

- Gelkopf M, Sigal M, Kremer R. The use of humor for improving social support in a psychiatric ward. *The Journal of Social Psychology*. 1994;134:175–182.

- Gelkopf M, Kreitler S. Is humor only fun, an alternative cure or magic? The cognitive therapeutic potential of humor. *Journal of Cognitive Psychotherapy*. 1996;10(4):235–254.

- Gelkopf, Marc. The Use of Humor in Serious Mental Illness: A Review Evidence Based Complement Alt Med. 2011: 342837.
  https://www.hindawi.com/journals/ecam/2011/342837/

- Lefcourt HM, Davidson K, Prkachin KM, Mills DE. Humor

as a stress moderator in the prediction of blood pressure obtained during five stressful tasks. *Journal of Research in Personality*. 1997;31(4):523–542.

- Richman J. The lifesaving function of humor with the depressed and suicidal elderly. *Gerontologist*. 1995;35(2):271–273.

- Sultanoff SM. Integrating humor into psychotherapy. In: Schaefer C, editor. *Play Therapy with Adults*. New York: John and Sons; 2003. pp. 107–143.

- Sultanoff, S. Assorted published articles available at www.humormatters.com. Topics include Humor and Health, Humor in the Workplace, Humor and Resilience, Using Humor In Crisis, Humor and Heart Disease, Using Humor in Counseling, The Research on Humor, and more.

- Ventis WL, Higbee G, Murdock SA. Using humor in systematic desensitization to reduce fear. *Journal of General Psychology*. 2001;128(2):241–253.

- Walter M, Hänni B, Haug M, et al. Humour therapy in patients with late-life depression or Alzheimer's disease: a pilot study. *International Journal of Geriatric Psychiatry*. 2007;22(1)

Contact Information:

David Jacobson   humorhorizon@gmail.com

www.ingramcontent.com/pod-product-compliance
Lightning Source LLC
Chambersburg PA
CBHW071342290326
41933CB00040B/2089